AF228954

WOMEN IN
Fashion

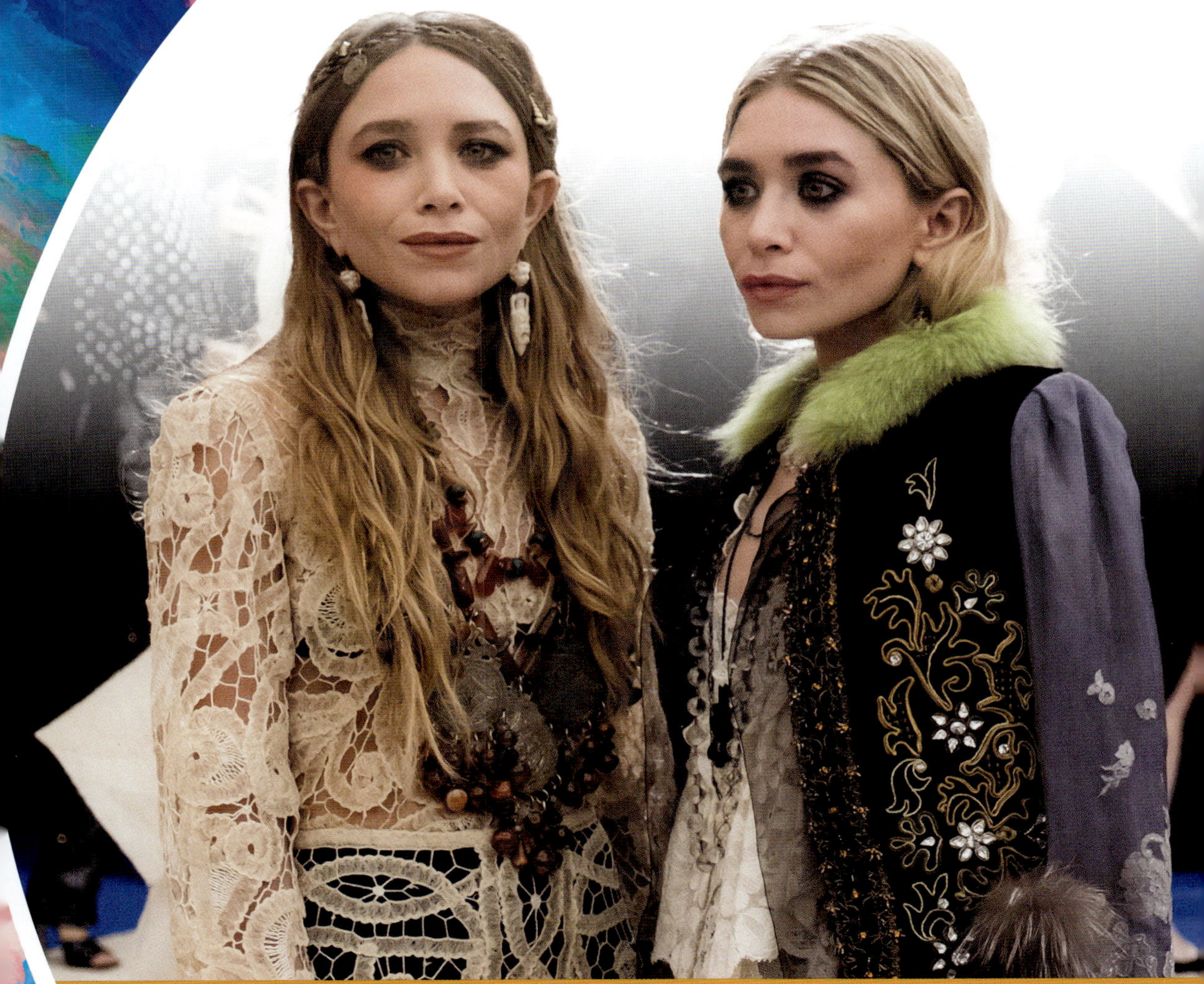

BY WENDY HINOTE LANIER

CONTENT CONSULTANT
Elizabeth Kessler
American Studies Program Coordinator
Stanford University

Cover image: Mary-Kate, *left*, and Ashley Olsen are influential fashion designers.

Core Library

An Imprint of Abdo Publishing
abdopublishing.com

abdopublishing.com

Published by Abdo Publishing, a division of ABDO, PO Box 398166, Minneapolis, Minnesota 55439. Copyright © 2019 by Abdo Consulting Group, Inc. International copyrights reserved in all countries. No part of this book may be reproduced in any form without written permission from the publisher. Core Library™ is a trademark and logo of Abdo Publishing.

Printed in the United States of America, North Mankato, Minnesota
022018
092018

Cover Photo: Charles Sykes/Invision/AP Images
Interior Photos: Charles Sykes/Invision/AP Images, 1; Leonard Zhukovsky/Shutterstock Images, 4–5; Genevieve de Manio/Getty Images News/Getty Images, 8; Hulton-Deutsch Collection/ Corbis Historical/Getty Images, 12–13; Maja Hitij/picture alliance/dpa/AP Images, 15, 43; Chicago History Museum/Archive Photos/Getty Images, 19 (left); Staff Mirrorpix/Newscom, 19 (middle left); Mirrorpix/Newscom, 19 (middle); Richard Rutledge/Condé Nast Collection/Getty Images, 19 (middle right); Mirrorpix/Newscom, 19 (right); Patrick Demarchelier/Conde Nast/Contour Style/ Getty Images, 22–23; Shutterstock Images, 26; Sam Aronov/Shutterstock Images, 29; MEGA/ Newscom, 32–33; Red Line Editorial, 35; Andy Holzman/ZumaPress/Newscom, 39, 45; Dietrich Zeigler/Shutterstock Images, 40

Editor: Marie Pearson
Imprint Designer: Maggie Villaume
Series Design Direction: Claire Vanden Branden

Library of Congress Control Number: 2017962831

Publisher's Cataloging-in-Publication Data

Names: Lanier, Wendy Hinote, author.
Title: Women in fashion / by Wendy Hinote Lanier.
Description: Minneapolis, Minnesota : Abdo Publishing, 2019. | Series: Women in the arts | Includes online resources and index.
Identifiers: ISBN 9781532114748 (lib.bdg.) | ISBN 9781532154577 (ebook)
Subjects: LCSH: Women fashion designers--Juvenile literature. | Models (Persons-- Juvenile literature. | Fashion--History--Juvenile literature. | Fashion and art-- Juvenile literature.
Classification: DDC 746.920--dc23

CONTENTS

Vera Wang's Fashion Empire

era Wang is one of the most recognized names in fashion today. Wang's company began as an exclusive wedding gown label. Since 1990 her business has grown into a billion-dollar empire. It now includes clothing, china, shoes, mattresses, luggage, fragrances, and accessories such as jewelry and handbags.

PASSION FOR FASHION

Wang is the daughter of successful immigrants from China. Her love of fashion comes from her mother, who loved to visit shops in Paris, France. Wang often accompanied her on these

Wang was the youngest fashion editor for *Vogue* magazine when she started at age 23.

shopping trips. As a result, Wang grew to love clothing and the fashion industry.

After college Wang landed a job at *Vogue*, a fashion magazine. Eventually she became a senior fashion editor. Later she worked as a design director for Ralph Lauren. Her experiences taught her the fashion business from the inside out. But in her heart, she always knew she wanted to create her own designs.

THE START OF IT ALL

In 1989 Wang was getting married. She looked everywhere for a modern, sophisticated wedding dress. Frustrated and unable to find the look she wanted, Wang designed her own. Actually, she designed seven. Wang's experience told her there was a market that needed to be met. The next year, Wang's father provided the funds for her to launch her own line of wedding dresses.

Wang's first bridal boutique was a two-story shop space inside the Carlyle Hotel in Manhattan, New York City. She sold other famous designers' bridal gowns as well as her own. It wasn't long before Wang's business began to grow. People loved Wang's elegant gowns with an updated, edgy flair. By the mid-1990s, Wang was firmly established as a successful bridal gown designer.

THE NEXT STEP

From the beginning, Wang saw bridal wear as the foundation for her fashion business. Soon she branched out to evening wear. She was among the first to use illusion fabric in her designs. In the past, it had mainly

been used for bridal gowns. At a distance, the fabric looks like skin. It creates a revealing style without actually exposing too much. In 2000, Wang launched a successful ready-to-wear line that was both practical and fashionable.

Today Wang continues to expand her influence in the fashion world. Her brand now includes accessories, fragrances, and housewares, along with her clothing lines. At one time, only the rich could afford a

Wang trained as a figure skater growing up. She and a partner competed in the 1968 and 1969 US National Championships. But Wang never skated in the Olympics. Instead she has designed costumes for other skaters. In 1994 she designed an elegant costume for her friend Nancy Kerrigan. Kerrigan won an Olympic silver medal wearing a Vera Wang skating dress. It was made with illusion fabric and covered in rhinestones. Wang's design was so popular that it changed the look of figure skating from that point on.

Famous people including author and activist Chelsea Clinton have worn Vera Wang dresses for their weddings.

Vera Wang design. Now she has lines that are more affordable. Some department stores carry a Vera Wang fast fashion line. And even brides on a budget can purchase a Vera Wang dress through a national bridal store chain.

The fashion industry is highly competitive. Wang has become a success because she has worked hard. But she is not the first. Many women came before her. Some have become famous. Today many people are familiar with female designers. The labels on many of the most popular designs carry their names. Vera Wang is just one among many.

STRAIGHT TO THE
SOURCE

In December 2010, Wang discussed her early design work in an interview:

> But all the years I was designing, it frustrated me that I could reach so few women. . . . So my being able to reach the masses was something that meant a great deal to me—especially for women who could never wear Vera Wang. I used to get tons of letters that said, 'I'll never get to wear you,' or 'I'll never get married in one of your dresses,' or 'I'll never have an evening gown like the one I saw on the red carpet.' I thought that was sad, because you give your life to this and you end up reaching very few people. So that was a major goal for me—to be able to reach and encourage more women, to encourage them to express themselves and be what they want to be.

> Source: Evan Lysacek. "Vera Wang." *Interview Magazine.* Interview Magazine, December 15, 2010. Web. Accessed October 3, 2017.

What's the Big Idea?

Read the passage above carefully. What is the main point that Wang is making about her early years of designing? Why did the letters she received make her sad? What goal do you think she set for herself? Do you think she has achieved it?

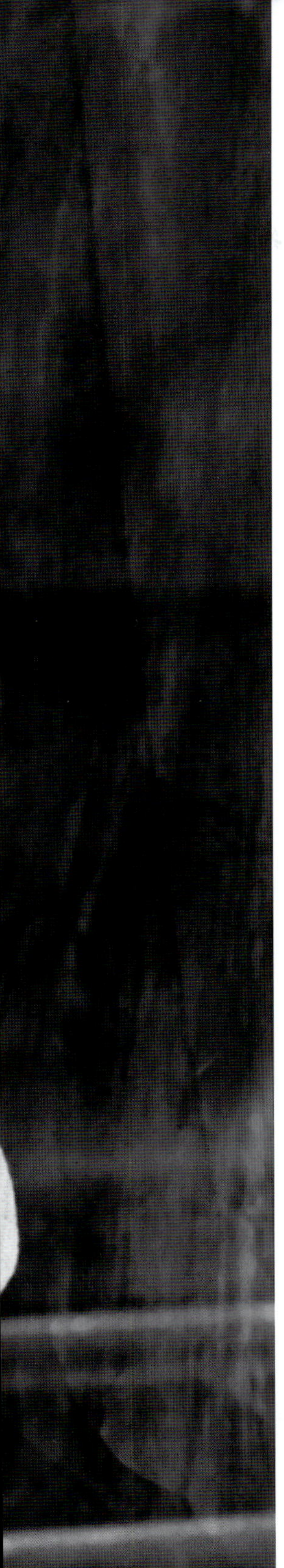

Fashion Pioneers

Early women's fashion designers were dressmakers. They were usually women. Yet by the mid-1800s, most famous designers were men. Women still worked as seamstresses, saleswomen, and apprentices. However, most designers worked under someone else's name. The names on the labels were mostly men's. But in the early 1900s, women designers started receiving credit for their work.

COCO CHANEL

The first world-famous women fashion designers were from Paris. Among them was

Designer Coco Chanel's name is still iconic today.

the legendary Gabrielle "Coco" Chanel. Chanel began her fashion career when she opened her first millinery shop in Paris in 1910. Her hats were popular with women of fashionable society. Chanel soon opened two more shops. She expanded her business to include clothing. Her clothing line included the use of a jersey knit fabric. This fabric made clothes less formal and more comfortable to wear. Some of her clothes were inspired by menswear. This is where she came up with the idea to use tweed, a woolen fabric she used to make jackets, skirts, and suits.

In 1922 Chanel introduced her famous Chanel No. 5 perfume. In 1925 she debuted the collarless cardigan jacket. It drew from button-down sweaters called cardigans. The jacket later became a popular piece for former First Lady Jacqueline Kennedy. And in 1926, Chanel introduced the "little black dress." At the time, black was usually worn when a loved one died. But Chanel's simple long-sleeved dress made black the must-have color for evening wear.

World War II (1939–1945) and unwise personal choices by Chanel interrupted her fashion career. But she made a comeback in the 1950s. In 1955, she created the still-famous quilted shoulder bag with a gold chain. This allowed a woman's hands to remain free while still carrying her purse. She introduced pea coats, which are heavy wool jackets, and bell-bottomed pants for women. Chanel died in 1971. Her design house and influence live on.

ELSA SCHIAPARELLI

In the 1920s, Elsa Schiaparelli arrived on the fashion scene in Paris. Schiap, as she was known, was already designing clothes for her friends and herself. In 1927 Schiap introduced a black sweater with a white bow knitted into the neckline. It was a huge success. She became famous overnight.

Schiap was a competitor of Chanel, but their styles were very different. Schiap's designs were both shocking and humorous. She used bold, contrasting colors, patterns, and funny decorations. She made clothes art. She embraced the popular artists of her day. Like them, she used everyday objects in unusual ways in her designs.

Schiap introduced a split skirt for a tennis outfit. The skirt was an early form of shorts. She used zippers and metal clips in place of buttons. Her designs were artistic and fun. They were also practical.

CLAIRE MCCARDELL

American designers in the early 1900s did not always receive credit for their work. Their designs often carried someone else's name. Most clothing with a person's name on it was from France. In the United States, Claire McCardell started designing in the late 1920s. She broke the mold by insisting her designs carry her name. As a result, she was one of the first American designers to become a household name.

McCardell is known as the creator of the American Look fashion style. Her designs included everything from evening dresses to swimsuits and play clothes made up of shorts and loose shirts. They were stylish but casual. They were comfortable and allowed women to move more freely than other styles. She was among the first to design separates that could be mixed. This allowed women to travel with fewer clothes.

From the start, McCardell wanted to create affordable ready-to-wear clothes. She pioneered the use of denim, cotton calico, and fasteners such as zippers for clothing. Her work became one of the most popular looks of the 1940s.

ANN LOWE

Ann Lowe was a pioneering African-American designer. She grew up in a family that made ball gowns for wealthy women in the South. Lowe went to New York City in 1917. She attended design school. After graduating she started a dress salon in Tampa, Florida. It quickly became the leading salon in the city.

In 1928 Lowe returned to New York City. She designed clothing for major stores and salons. But it was always under the names of others. In 1946 actress Olivia de Havilland wore an Ann Lowe gown to accept an award for her role in the film *To Each His Own*. The gown did not carry Lowe's name. Lowe was working with two challenges. Few designers of the day worked

FASHION ACROSS THE DECADES

The above timeline shows major fashion trends from the 1920s to the 1960s. How many of these trends did you find mentioned in the text? Are there some listed here that you did not find in the text? With help from an adult, do an Internet search on a decade to find out more about its fashion trends.

under their own names. And there were almost no African-American designers.

In 1953 Lowe designed an ivory silk wedding gown with appliqué flowers. The gown was for Jacqueline Bouvier, who was marrying then-Senator John F. Kennedy. The dress was known and loved throughout the world, but Lowe's name was not.

Still, she worked hard. In the late 1960s, she opened another salon in New York City. She became one of the first African-American designers to make a name for herself there.

MARY QUANT

British designer Mary Quant opened her own store in London, England, in 1955. She and her clients were young and looking for affordable, modern fashions. They wanted something different from what their mothers wore. Quant began stocking her store with her own designs to meet the demand. She created white knee-high lace-up boots and skinny sweaters in stripes and checks. Next, she designed sweaters and dresses with shiny white plastic collars. This reflected a change in the way people viewed fashion. They no longer expected clothing to be made of the finest materials. Quant's designs were wildly popular with young girls all over the world.

Quant was possibly the most influential designer of the 1960s. She is best known for introducing the miniskirt. Her short dresses and skirts in vibrant colors worn with printed tights became the look of the 1960s. She named the short garments minis after her favorite car, the Morris Mini. In later years, she continued to design household goods, makeup, and clothes.

Explore Online

Chapter Two talks about some of the great female designers of women's fashion. The website below discusses women who have changed the way people view fashion. What new information did you learn about the women in Chapter Two?

Fashionista: 25 Women Designers Who Changed Fashion Forever
abdocorelibrary.com/women-in-fashion

CHAPTER
THREE

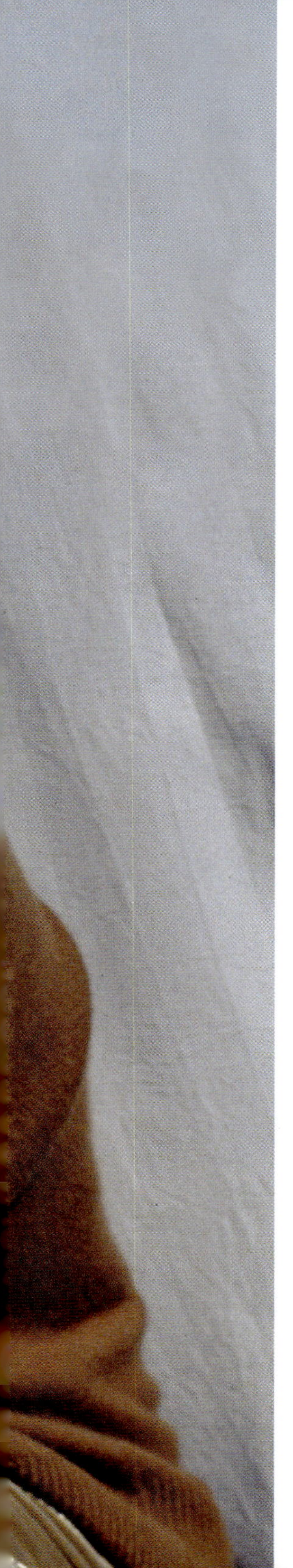

Recreating Fashion

In the late 1900s, many women designers became household names. They established their own design houses and developed multimillion-dollar businesses. They also expanded their brands to include more than clothing.

DONNA KARAN

In the late 1960s, designer Anne Klein hired Donna Karan, who had been a student at Parsons School of Design in New York City. By 1971 Karan was promoted to associate designer. After Klein's death in 1974, Karan

Vogue featured a Donna Karan cashmere sweater in a 1989 magazine.

became head designer. She left Anne Klein in 1984 to start her own label. Karan presented her first collection for women in 1985 under the label DK.

The DK collection featured Seven Easy Pieces, designed to take modern women from day to evening. The basic piece was a black bodysuit. Additional pieces could be added or changed to create different looks. These included a skirt, a pair of loose trousers, a tailored jacket, a sweater, a little black dress, and a white shirt. The sweater is known as the Cozy. It is usually made of cashmere. This thin sweater jacket has extra fabric panels. It can be tied or wrapped 12 ways. The Seven Easy Pieces changed with time. Other pieces were added.

Karan continued to develop her brand throughout the late 1900s and into the 2000s. In 1988 she rolled out a less expensive DK line. It was called Donna Karan New York (DKNY). In 1990 she created DKNY jeans. They were an instant hit. In 1992 she introduced her first perfume. And in 2007, Karan introduced the Urban Zen brand. The clothes draw from African and Haitian styles. They are made to be worn year-round. Karan's vision for Urban Zen is to promote health care, education, and cultural preservation in less-developed countries.

DIANE VON FURSTENBERG

Belgian-born Diane von Furstenberg burst on the New York fashion scene in the early 1970s. She showed her first collection in 1970. In 1972 she opened a showroom on Seventh Avenue. She designed several pieces using a jersey knit fabric that included a wrap top and a matching

Fashion Design School

Most of today's top designers spend at least some time in design school. Many state universities offer programs in fashion. There are also entire schools dedicated to the art of design. The Fashion Institute of Design and Merchandising is located in California. The Savannah College of Art and Design has two locations in Georgia. And the Fashion Institute of Technology and Parsons School of Design are both in New York City.

skirt. Then she saw a woman on television wearing the wrap top and skirt together. She realized they could be made into a dress. Soon after, she introduced her signature wrap dress. The wrap dress was a comfortable business dress that could be worn into the evening. This versatility was important as more women entered the workforce.

The wrap dress had a bias-cut skirt, low neckline, strong collar, and cuffs. It was the first dress of its kind made of jersey. By 1976 von Furstenberg had sold more than 5 million of them. In the 1990s, she expanded her brand to include ready-to-wear, handbags, shoes, small leather goods, scarves, and fine jewelry. Today von Furstenberg often mentors young designers.

MIUCCIA PRADA

Miuccia Prada's grandfather established the family's leather-goods company in 1913. Prada joined the business in 1970. She introduced leather-trimmed nylon backpacks. The waterproof bags were an instant hit.

In 1979 Prada inherited the family company. Under her leadership, it began making high-quality handbags. Then in 1989, she launched her first clothing collection. She continued to build her label, creating clothing with clean, simple lines. They were made of luxury fabrics in basic colors and were tailored and modest. The style became a favorite with well-to-do working women. In 1993 Prada introduced Miu Miu. The more affordable brand is aimed at a younger crowd. Miu Miu offers a sharp contrast to Prada's usual pieces. It includes bright colors and bold patterns. Both collections have helped make her company a huge success.

TRACY REESE

As children, Tracy Reese and her sisters liked to sew. She didn't know it then, but her career was being built through a favorite family activity. After taking a Parsons School of Design summer program, Reese enrolled there full-time. She earned her degree in 1984. Reese immediately took a job as an apprentice to French designer Martine Sitbon. Reese launched her first label in 1987. Her designs were well received. But Reese struggled to keep the business afloat. She was forced to close in 1989. She was only 23 years old.

Reese regularly shows her work during New York Fashion Week.

Reese worked in high-end fashion houses for the next few years. While there she learned the business of fashion. In 1995 Reese made a deal with The Limited—an American clothing company—to produce her own line. Its success gave her the funds she needed to start her own label.

Fashion Week is a series of fashion shows. The most important ones are held in New York City, New York; London, United Kingdom; Milan, Italy; and Paris, France. In the United States, the shows run in February and September. Designers introduce their newest styles to buyers, the press, and the public. In the past, the shows announced the coming fashions. But social media has brought a few changes. Now some styles on the runway are available for immediate purchase. It is a sign of success for designers to showcase their work at Fashion Week.

In 1996 Reese launched a sportswear line called Tracy Reese Meridian. The name was later shortened to Tracy Reese. In 1998 she introduced a line for younger customers called Plenty. By 2002 Reese was a successful designer. Her designs use bright colors and have a polished, feminine look. In 2012 Reese designed a custom outfit for then-First Lady Michelle Obama.

STRAIGHT TO THE
SOURCE

Diane von Furstenberg came to the United States in 1969. She brought a suitcase full of sample dresses with her. By the time she was 29, she had established herself as a designer. Von Furstenberg discussed her success in her book *The Woman I Wanted to Be*:

> *When young people eager to start their own lives and careers ask me for advice I smile and always say: "Passion and persistence are what matter. Dreams are achievable and you can make your fantasy come true, but there are no shortcuts. Nothing happens without hard work."*
>
> *That advice is the essence of my journey with the little dresses when I arrived in New York. . . . The people I met were amused and intrigued by the unorthodox presentation of little jersey dresses pulled out of a Vuitton suitcase . . . but it did not materialize into anything. I persevered, though.*
>
> Source: Diane von Furstenberg. *The Woman I Wanted to Be.* New York: Simon & Schuster, 2014. Print. 154–155.

Changing Minds

In this passage, von Furstenberg gives advice about what she believes is necessary for success. What does she say are the keys to achieving your dreams? Do you agree? Why or why not?

CHAPTER
FOUR

The New Guard

Many of today's top designers have been creating fashion for more than 25 years. Some designers have turned their focus to projects outside of fashion. Others are retiring. Now a new group of designers is moving to the forefront of the fashion world.

MARY-KATE AND ASHLEY OLSEN

Mary-Kate and Ashley Olsen are frequently listed among today's most influential designers. The twins left their careers as child actresses behind them to become stars in the world of fashion design.

Ashley, *left*, and Mary-Kate Olsen wore clothing from one of their lines to the 2017 Council of Fashion Designers of America Fashion Awards.

The Olsens introduced The Row in 2006. The Row is a high-end luxury brand. It includes ready-to-wear, eyewear, handbags, and shoes. The Row designs have included loose white shirts, long dark coats, and elegant loose pants. Each season brings a new look. The Olsens have proved to be trendsetters. They make simple, quality clothes. Their focus on fine fabrics and the perfect fit has earned them high praise. The sisters were Council of Fashion Designers of America's Womenswear Designers of the Year in 2012 and 2015.

In 2007 the sisters introduced a vintage-inspired collection called Elizabeth and James. The Olsens describe the line as all about balance. They try to balance formal pieces with more casual ones. They balance feminine pieces with looks inspired by menswear. The line is intended to make women feel confident and effortless.

In 2009 the Olsens released a stylish but affordable line called Olsenboye for a large department store.

FASHION EMPLOYMENT

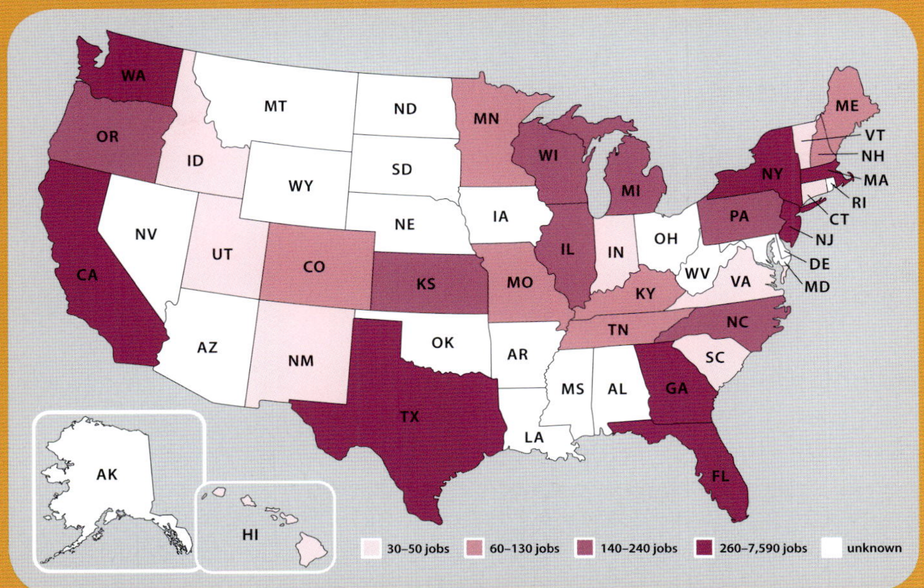

Most fashion design jobs are in big cities. This map shows how many fashion designers work in each state. Why do you think some of these states have more designers than others?

The designs draw inspiration from teen trends around the world. It mixes fancy with casual. Some Olsenboye designs have included an army jacket with studs and gray jeans.

CHLOE DAO

Chloe Dao was born in Laos. She came to the United States when she was eight years old. Her family settled in Houston, Texas. At age 20, Dao went to New York City to attend the Fashion Institute of Technology. She spent eight years in New York, earning a degree and working in the fashion industry.

In 2000 Dao returned to Houston. She opened her own boutique. Originally known as Lot 8, the store is now called DAO Chloe DAO. It is stocked with Dao's own sportswear, evening wear, and bridal collection. She also carries designs by other Houston designers and some New York designers.

In 2005 Dao participated in the television fashion competition show *Project Runway*. She was crowned the winner of Season 2. Since then Dao has become an international fashion superstar and continues to expand her fashion brand. She has designed travel accessories and developed a line for a home shopping network. She is also active in Houston community service. Her feminine and flattering designs regularly receive rave reviews.

CECILIA CASSINI

Latina designer Cecilia Cassini is known as the "Mozart of Fashion." Like the famed composer of the 1700s, Cassini started at a young age. She began designing at age four when she started cutting up clothing and reusing the material. By the time she was ten in 2009, Cassini was making a name for herself. She introduced her label. It began attracting national attention early on. She has designed clothes for celebrities including Taylor Swift.

Cassini's signature look includes brightly colored patterned dresses decorated with ruffles and bows of all sizes. Her one-of-a-kind

Project Runway

Project Runway is a reality television show for aspiring fashion designers. In 2017 the show completed its 16th season. Each week participants on the show create pieces to meet a design challenge. At the end of each challenge, one designer is eliminated. The winner of *Project Runway* receives funds to start his or her own line, in addition to other opportunities. A few *Project Runway* winners have gone on to successful fashion careers.

girls' clothing is sold through a California store and her website. Cassini balances school and design work by making sure all homework is done at school. Her time at home is filled with sewing and creating new designs.

CUSHNIE ET OCHS

Carly Cushnie and business partner Michelle Ochs were classmates at Parsons School of Design. While still in school, they teamed up to create their own line. Their senior collections generated a lot of attention. After graduating in 2008, the women launched their own design label.

At ten years old, Cassini was designing clothes for children.

The label, Cushnie et Ochs, is known for its sleek, tailored cutout dresses. The look is sophisticated and modern. The designers have earned a huge following. Their clients include celebrities and famous people such as Jennifer Lopez. In 2018, Ochs left the company.

Cushnie continued to work on the label, which kept its name.

INTO THE FUTURE

At the start of the 1900s, most women designed and made their own clothes. But throughout the 1900s, women created fashion empires. They took on important roles in fashion earlier than in other industries. In the 2000s, new designers are stepping into the spotlight. They design clothing, jewelry, perfume, and accessories with their names on the label. Women are the driving force behind today's fashion industry.

Further Evidence

Part of Chapter Four summarizes Chloe Dao's career. What was the main point of this section? Go to the website below. What evidence in the interview do you find that supports the Dao section of the chapter? Does the article offer any additional information?

Visit Houston: Chloe Dao

abdocorelibrary.com/women-in-fashion

NOTABLE WORKS

The Little Black Dress—Coco Chanel

Before Chanel introduced her little black dress in 1926, black was usually worn when mourning the death of a loved one. But Chanel's simple long-sleeved dress could be worn during the day or evening. Simply changing the hat, gloves, or jewelry changed the look of the entire dress. By the end of the 1920s, it was a favorite uniform for the fashionable woman.

Seven Easy Pieces—Donna Karan

In 1985 Karan made life simpler for women everywhere when she introduced her Seven Easy Pieces. The wardrobe began with a black bodysuit. The bodysuit served as a foundation for a variety of looks. Six other pieces could be interchanged to make different outfits. Through the years, Karan refined the collection by redesigning certain pieces or adding other pieces such as a large scarf.

The Wrap Dress—Diane von Furstenberg

Von Furstenberg realized jersey knit fabrics could be used to make flattering and comfortable clothes. In the early 1970s, she made a wrap top and matching skirt into a dress. In 1974 she debuted a wrap dress with a low neckline, strong collar, and cuffs.

The Row—Mary-Kate and Ashley Olsen

The Row is a high-end design house founded in 2006 by former child stars Mary-Kate and Ashley Olsen. The brand emphasizes high-end manufacturing in the United States. The sisters have won Womenswear Designers of the Year honors twice for this line.

STOP AND THINK

Dig Deeper

After reading this book, what questions do you still have about women in fashion design? With an adult's help, find a few reliable sources that can help you answer your questions. Write a paragraph about what you learned.

Take a Stand

This book talks about designing clothes that are expensive for a few people or inexpensive and available to the masses. Do you think a fashion designer should focus on making clothes that many people can enjoy or for a narrower market? Why?

Why Do I Care?

Not everyone cares about what they wear, but some people think that their clothing is a means of self-expression. Do you wear clothes as a way to express yourself? Does what you wear affect the way you feel or boost your confidence? Why or why not?

Surprise Me

Chapter Two of this book talks about some of the pioneers in women's fashion. What two or three facts about these women did you find most surprising? Write a few sentences about each fact. Why did you find each fact surprising?

GLOSSARY

appliqué
a decoration or trimming made of one material that is sewn or glued to another material

boutique
a shop or store that sells specialty items such as clothing or gifts

fast fashion
a term used to describe trendy clothing that moves quickly from the fashion shows to the retailers

jersey knit
a soft cloth woven out of materials such as cotton or wool

mentor
to guide or help

millinery
hats and trimmings sold by a milliner or hat maker

ready-to-wear
factory-made clothing sold in standard sizes

salon
a business or shop that offers a specific service or product, usually related to fashion

twin sets
sweater sets that include a matching pullover sweater and button-down sweater

vintage
high-quality look or style of the past

ONLINE RESOURCES

To learn more about women in fashion, visit our free resource websites below.

Visit **abdocorelibrary.com** for free Common Core resources for teachers and students, including vetted activities, multimedia, and booklinks, for deeper subject comprehension.

Visit **abdobooklinks.com** for free additional online weblinks for further learning. These links are routinely monitored and updated to provide the most current information available.

LEARN MORE

Albee, Sarah. *Why'd They Wear That? Fashion as the Mirror of History*. Washington, DC: National Geographic, 2015.

Felix, Rebecca. *Mary Quant: Miniskirt Maker*. Minneapolis, MN: Abdo, 2018.

INDEX

About the Author

Wendy Hinote Lanier is a native Texan and former elementary teacher who writes and speaks for children and adults on a variety of topics. She is the author of more than 25 books for children and young adults.